Like us on Facebook
@RiddlesandGiggles

Follow us on Instagram
@RiddlesandGiggles_Official

Questions & Customer Service
hello@riddlesandgiggles.com

Christmas Knock Knock Joke Book for Kids
by Riddles and Giggles™
www.riddlesandgiggles.com

© 2021 Riddles and Giggles™

All rights reserved. This book or parts thereof may not be reproduced in any form, stored in any retrieval system, or transmitted in any form by any means—electronic, mechanical, photocopy, recording, or otherwise—without prior written permission of the publisher, except as provided by United States of America copyright law. For permissions contact: hello@riddlesandgiggles.com

Not for resale. All books, digital products, eBooks and PDF downloads are subject to copyright protection. Each book, eBook and PDF download is licensed to a single user only. Customers are not allowed to copy, distribute, share and/or transfer the product they have purchased to any third party.

FREE BONUS

Get your FREE book download

Christmas Jokes & Would You Rather for Kids

- Contains a collection of cracking Christmas jokes and Would You Rather Christmas-themed questions

- More endless giggles and entertainment for the whole family.

Claim your FREE book at www.riddlesandagiggles.com/christmas

Or scan with your phone to get your free download

TABLE OF CONTENTS

Welcome... 4
  1. Names 7
  2. Santa & His Helpers... 19
  3. Christmas Carols.. 27
  4. Christmas Decorations & Traditions 37
  5. Christmas Gifts 43
  6. Christmas Dinner & Festivities 53
  7. New Year Celebrations...................................... 65
  8. Winter Fun 69
Before You Go 79
References 102

WELCOME

Hi there, Jokester!

Knock-knock jokes are a great way for people to have fun and share laughs together.

Lots of people love to tell knock-knock jokes. Some are very funny. Some are just corny. Other knock-knock jokes make no sense at all. One thing we can agree on about knock-knock jokes is that kids love them!

I hope you are one of those kids, because if you want a collection of funny, corny, and laugh-out-loud knock-knock jokes, then this book is for you!

The *Christmas Knock Knock Joke Book for Kids* is an awesome collection of good, clean, fun knock-knock jokes that will make you roll your eyes, snort, giggle, groan, and laugh out loud.

You can read this whole book or pick which knock-knock jokes you want to read in any order you want.

You can also enjoy reading the knock-knock jokes on your own or share the jokes with everyone around you. Or you can take turns reading the knock-knock jokes out loud with family and friends.

So, grab your Christmas treats and get ready for some funny and corny Christmas knock-knock jokes!

PSST... You can also color the Christmas pictures to use this book as a coloring book AND a joke book!

Tips on How to Tell a Knock-Knock Joke

- Practice reading the joke out loud a few times to help you remember it. You may want to practice reading in front of a mirror.
- Find a family member or friend and ask them if they want to hear a knock-knock joke.
- As you tell the joke, remember to say it slowly and clearly so people understand every word.
- Adding a small pause helps to build up suspense and can make the joke even funnier.
- Deliver the final punch line. Remember to say it slowly, then wait for the laughs.
- If you mess up, that's OK. Move on and tell another joke. Remember, everyone loves knock-knock jokes!

NAMES

Knock, knock.
Who's there?
Chris.
Chris who?
Christmas is here!

Knock, knock.
Who's there?
Ivana.
Ivana who?
Ivana wish you a
Merry Christmas.

Knock, knock.
Who's there?
Harriet.
Harriet who?
"Harriet up," said the elf.
"It's almost Christmas!"

Knock, knock.
Who's there?
Harmony.
Harmony who?
Harmony days left
until Christmas?

Knock, knock.
Who's there?
Howie.
Howie who?
Howie going to sleep? I'm too excited about Christmas.

Knock, knock.
Who's there?
Ben.
Ben who?
Ben waiting all day to hang up the stockings.

Knock, knock.
Who's there?
Claus.
Claus who?
Claus I can't wait any longer.

Knock, knock.
Who's there?
Murray.
Murray who?
Murray Christmas,
one and all.

Knock, knock.
Who's there?
Shirley.
Shirley who?
Shirley you put your
Christmas stocking out?

Knock, knock.
Who's there?
Allie.
Allie who?
Allie want for
Christmas is you.

Knock, knock.
Who's there?
Amelia.
Amelia who?
Amelia letter to
the North Pole for
Santa today.

Knock, knock.
Who's there?
Holly.
Holly who?
Holly-days are
here again!

Knock, knock.
Who's there?
Phillip.
Phillip who?
Phillip my stocking with
candy and toys, please!

Knock, knock.
Who's there?
Toby.
Toby who?
Toby on the Santa's nice
list, you must be good.

Knock, knock.
Who's there?
Avery.
Avery who?
Avery Merry
Christmas to you.

Knock, knock.
Who's there?
Luke.
Luke who?
Luke at the amazing Christmas decorations!

Knock, knock.
Who's there?
Frankie.
Frankie who?
Frankie-cense, gold, and myrrh.

Knock, knock.
Who's there?
Isabelle.
Isabelle who?
Isabelle ringing?

Knock, knock.
Who's there?
Harry.
Harry who?
Harry up and open your gift!

Knock, knock.
Who's there?
Evan.
Evan who?
Evan the elves don't know what Santa's brought them for Christmas.

Knock, knock.
Who's there?
Cole.
Cole who?
Cole is not what I was expecting in my stocking this year.

Knock, knock.
Who's there?
Anna.
Anna who?
Anna partridge in a pear tree.

Knock, knock.
Who's there?
Emma.
Emma who?
Emma really hungry; I can't wait for Christmas dinner.

Knock, knock.
Who's there?
Anita.
Anita who?
Anita another bow for this present.

Knock, knock.
Who's there?
Colleen.
Colleen who?
Colleen your room or you'll be on the naughty list.

Knock, knock.
Who's there?
Alex.
Alex who?
Alex my mom who's coming over for Christmas dinner.

Knock, knock.
Who's there?
Gladys.
Gladys who?
Gladys not me who got coal in their stocking.

Knock, knock.
Who's there?
Robin.
Robin who?
"Robin all the Christmas presents this year too," said the Grinch.

Knock, knock.
Who's there?
Howard.
Howard who?
Howard you like to sing Christmas carols with me?

NAMES

Knock, knock.
Who's there?
Noah.
Noah who?
Noah body loves Christmas as much as I do.

Knock, knock.
Who's there?
Candy.
Candy who?
Candy Grinch really steal Christmas?

Knock, knock.
Who's there?
Esther.
Esther who?
Esther any figgy pudding for dessert?

Knock, knock.
Who's there?
Arthur.
Arthur who?
Arthur any pies left?

Knock, knock.
Who's there?
Ginger.
Ginger who?
Ginger bread is my favorite bread.

Knock, knock.
Who's there?
Jimmy.
Jimmy who?
Jimmy a kiss under the mistletoe.

Knock, knock.
Who's there?
Tamara.
Tamara who?
Tamara we will have to clean up all this wrapping paper!

Knock, knock.
Who's there?
Justin.
Justin who?
Justin time for warm Christmas cookies!

Knock, knock.
Who's there?
Candice.
Candice who?
Candice day get any better?

Knock, knock.
Who's there?
Mary and Abby.
Mary and Abby who?
Mary Christmas and an Abby New Year!

2

SANTA
& HIS HELPERS

Knock, knock.
Who's there?
Adore.
Adore who?
Adore is OK for Santa but he prefers going down the chimney!

Knock, knock.
Who's there?
Leaf.
Leaf who?
Leaf some cookies and milk out for Santa.

Knock, knock.
Who's there?
Gunner.
Gunner who?
Gunner visit the North Pole to see Santa's workshop.

Knock, knock.
Who's there?
Freeze.
Freeze who?
"Freeze a jolly good fellow. Freeze a jolly good fellow."

Knock, knock.
Who's there?
Howl.
Howl who?
Howl Santa know what you want for Christmas if you don't send him a letter?

Knock, knock.
Who's there?
Dewey.
Dewey who?
Dewey know how long until Santa arrives?

SANTA & HIS HELPERS

Knock, knock.
Who's there?
Kansas.
Kansas who?
Kansas be the right way
to the North Pole?

Knock, knock.
Who's there?
Orange.
Orange who?
Orange you glad you
were good all year?

Knock, knock.
Who's there?
Lion.
Lion who?
Lion will put you on Santa's naughty list.

Knock, knock.
Who's there?
Russian.
Russian who?
Russian to finish the toys in time for Christmas.

Knock, knock.
Who's there?
Alpaca.
Alpaca who?
Alpaca another present on the sleigh for Santa.

Knock, knock.
Who's there?
Hosanna.
Hosanna who?
Hosanna gonna fit down the chimney?

Knock, knock.
Who's there?
Coal.
Coal who?
Coal me if you hear
Santa coming.

Knock, knock.
Who's there?
Theodore.
Theodore who?
Theodore was locked, so
Santa used the chimney.

Knock, knock.
Who's there?
Elf.
Elf who?
Elf me wrap this
present for Santa!

Knock, knock.
Who's there?
Ida.
Ida who?
Ida seen Santa if I
hadn't fallen asleep.

SANTA & HIS HELPERS

Knock, knock.
Who's there?
Interrupting Santa.
Interrupting Santa who?
Inter– Ho ho ho! Merry Christmas!

Knock, knock.
Who's there?
Ho ho.
Ho ho who?
Your Santa impression certainly needs more work.

3

CHRISTMAS CAROLS

Knock, knock.
Who's there?
Allison.
Allison who?
Allison to Christmas carols all December long!

Knock, knock.
Who's there?
Honda.
Honda who?
"Honda first day of Christmas my true love sent to me…"

Knock, knock.
Who's there?
Allis.
Allis who?
"Allis calm, Allis bright."

Knock, knock.
Who's there?
Nun.
Nun who?
Nun of the other reindeer let poor Rudolph join in any reindeer games.

Knock, knock.
Who's there?
Dexter.
Dexter who?
"Dexter halls with boughs of holly..."

Knock, knock.
Who's there?
Dewey.
Dewey who?
Dewey really need to listen to more Christmas carols?

Knock, knock.
Who's there?
Olive.
Olive who?
"Olive the other reindeer used to laugh and call him names."

Knock, knock.
Who's there?
Thermos.
Thermos who?
"It's thermos wonderful time of the year."

Knock, knock.
Who's there?
Icy.
Icy who?
"Icy Mommy kissing Santa Claus."

Knock, knock.
Who's there?
Sea shoes.
Sea shoes who?
"He sea shoes when you're sleeping..."

Knock, knock.
Who's there?
Roxanne.
Roxanne who?
"Roxanne around the Christmas tree!"

Knock, knock.
Who's there?
Dew.
Dew who?
"Dew you hear
what I hear?"

Knock, knock.
Who's there?
Peas.
Peas who?
Peas come home
for Christmas.

Knock, knock.
Who's there?
Nana.
Nana who?
Nana the other
carolers sing like me.

Knock, knock.
Who's there?
Delane.
Delane who?
"In Delane, the snow
is glistening…"

Knock, knock.
Who's there?
Ura.
Ura who?
"He knows when
Ura wake..."

Knock, knock.
Who's there?
Guinea.
Guinea who?
"It's be-guinea to look
a lot like Christmas."

Knock, knock.
Who's there?
Dachshund.
Dachshund who?
"Dachshund through
the snow..."

Knock, knock.
Who's there?
Pizza.
Pizza who?
"Pizza on earth, good
will toward men!"

Knock, knock.
Who's there?
Donut.
Donut who?
Donut sing Christmas carols if you don't know the words!

Knock, knock.
Who's there?
Oakham.
Oakham who?
"Oakham all ye faithful…"

Knock, knock.
Who's there?
Oh Chris.
Oh Chris who?
"Oh Christmas tree, oh Christmas tree…"

Knock, knock.
Who's there?
Harold.
Harold who?
Harold angels sing, "Glory to the newborn king…"

Knock, knock.
Who's there?
Ima.
Ima who?
"Ima dreaming of a white Christmas."

Knock, knock.
Who's there?
Wayne.
Wayne who?
"Wayne in a manger…"

CHRISTMAS CAROLS

Knock, knock.
Who's there?
Hurdle.
Hurdle who?
Hurdle these Christmas carols already today.

Knock, knock.
Who's there?
Yusef.
Yusef who?
"Have Yusef a merry little Christmas."

Knock, knock.
Who's there?
Leaded.
Leaded who?
"Leaded snow, leaded snow, leaded snow!"

Knock, knock.
Who's there?
Tree.
Tree who?
"Tree French hens,
two turtle doves, and a
partridge in a pear tree..."

Knock, knock.
Who's there?
Icing.
Icing who?
Icing Christmas
carols pretty well!

CHRISTMAS DECORATIONS & TRADITIONS

Knock, knock.
Who's there?
Pudding.
Pudding who?
Pudding up the
Christmas decorations.

Knock, knock.
Who's there?
Norma Lee.
Norma Lee who?
Norma Lee I put the
star on top of the tree.

Knock, knock.
Who's there?
Kanye.
Kanye who?
Kanye help me untangle the Christmas lights?

Knock, knock.
Who's there?
Dishes.
Dishes who?
Dishes the perfect place to hang the Christmas wreath.

Knock, knock.
Who's there?
Candy.
Candy who?
Candy canes hanging on the Christmas tree.

Knock, knock.
Who's there?
Santa.
Santa who?
Santa Christmas card to you. Did you get it?

Knock, knock.
Who's there?
Shell.
Shell who?
Shell we go see the Christmas lights?

Knock, knock.
Who's there?
Sarah.
Sarah who?
Sarah reason you didn't decorate the tree?

Knock, knock.
Who's there?
Norway.
Norway who?
Norway am I kissing anyone under the mistletoe.

Knock, knock.
Who's there?
Angel.
Angel who?
Angel on top of our
Christmas tree.

Knock, knock.
Who's there?
Reefs.
Reefs who?
Reefs on the door look
nice at Christmas.

Knock, knock.
Who's there?
Roach.
Roach who?
Roach you a
Christmas card.

Knock, knock.
Who's there?
Kenya.
Kenya who?
Kenya get me some
candy canes?

Knock, knock.
Who's there?
Tennis.
Tennis who?
Tennis the number of candy canes I've hung on the Christmas tree.

Knock, knock.
Who's there?
Owl.
Owl who?
Owl say, that's a nice Christmas tree!

Knock, knock.
Who's there?
Sausage.
Sausage who?
Sausage a beautiful Christmas tree last night!

5

CHRISTMAS GIFTS

Knock, knock.
Who's there?
Butter.
Butter who?
Butter not open
this present before
Christmas!

Knock, knock.
Who's there?
Snow.
Snow who?
Snow use, I can't think
of anything to get
you for Christmas.

Knock, knock.
Who's there?
Pecan.
Pecan who?
Pecan at your gifts
is naughty.

Knock, knock.
Who's there?
Ken.
Ken who?
Ken you tell me what you
got inside your stocking?

Knock, knock.
Who's there?
Rhino.
Rhino who?
Rhino what you want
for Christmas.

Knock, knock.
Who's there?
Windmill.
Windmill who?
Windmill we open
presents?

CHRISTMAS GIFTS

Knock, knock.
Who's there?
Juno.
Juno who?
Juno where Mum and Dad are hiding all the presents?

Knock, knock.
Who's there?
General Lee.
General Lee who?
General Lee I don't wait to open my gifts.

Knock, knock.
Who's there?
Bed.
Bed who?
Bed you can't guess what I got for Christmas.

Knock, knock.
Who's there?
Annie.
Annie who?
Annie way we can start opening our presents early?

Knock, knock.
Who's there?
Tom Sawyer.
Tom Sawyer who?
Tom Sawyer Christmas present, and he loved it!

Knock, knock.
Who's there?
Narnia.
Narnia who?
Narnia business what I got you for Christmas.

Knock, knock.
Who's there?
Yah.
Yah who?
Wow, you're getting really excited about Christmas!

Knock, knock.
Who's there?
Wooden shoe.
Wooden shoe who?
Wooden shoe like to know what I got you for Christmas?

Knock, knock.
Who's there?
Pikachu.
Pikachu who?
Pikachu Christmas presents, and you'll be in trouble.

Knock, knock.
Who's there?
Rabbit.
Rabbit who?
Rabbit up neatly. It's a present for Nana.

Knock, knock.
Who's there?
Wanda.
Wanda who?
Wanda know what you're getting for Christmas?

Knock, knock.
Who's there?
Voodoo.
Voodoo who?
Voodoo you think has the best stocking?

Knock, knock.
Who's there?
Water.
Water who?
Water you waiting for? Let's open presents!

Knock, knock.
Who's there?
That's.
That's who?
That's a lot of gifts!

Knock, knock.
Who's there?
Tank.
Tank who?
You're welcome! I thought you'd like that present.

Knock, knock.
Who's there?
Alva.
Alva who?
Alva another gift for you!

Knock, knock.
Who's there?
Abbott.
Abbott who?
Abbott time for more presents?

Knock, knock.
Who's there?
Chicken.
Chicken who?
Chicken the stocking for candy.

CHRISTMAS GIFTS

MERRY CHRISTMAS!

6
CHRISTMAS DINNER & FESTIVITIES

Knock, knock.
Who's there?
Canoe.
Canoe who?
Canoe help me bake some Christmas cookies?

Knock, knock.
Who's there?
Yule.
Yule who?
Yule know when you answer the door.

Knock, knock.
Who's there?
Dino.
Dino who?
Dino what's on the menu
for Christmas dinner?

Knock, knock.
Who's there?
Heaven.
Heaven who?
Heaven seen you
since last Christmas.

Knock, knock.
Who's there?
Gopher.
Gopher who?
Gopher the ugliest
Christmas sweater
you can find!

Knock, knock.
Who's there?
June.
June who?
June know how long
until the turkey is
done? I'm hungry.

CHRISTMAS DINNER & FESTIVITIES

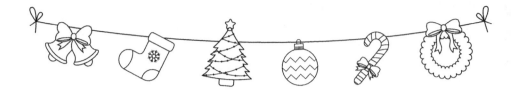

Knock, knock.
Who's there?
Rufus.
Rufus who?
Rufus falling off of your gingerbread house.

Knock, knock.
Who's there?
Lettuce.
Lettuce who?
Lettuce start eating. I'm starving!

Knock, knock.
Who's there?
Bacon.
Bacon who?
Bacon some Christmas cookies, and it smells yummy!

Knock, knock.
Who's there?
Cupper.
Cupper who?
Cupper hot cocoa would be nice.

Knock, knock.
Who's there?
Thumping.
Thumping who?
Thumping burning
in the oven?

Knock, knock.
Who's there?
Danby.
Danby who?
Danby late. Christmas
dinner starts at 6 pm.

Knock, knock.
Who's there?
Yuletide.
Yuletide who?
Yuletide yourself over
with a snack until dinner.

Knock, knock.
Who's there?
Jamaican.
Jamaican who?
Jamaican me hungry
with the smell of those
Christmas cookies.

Knock, knock.
Who's there?
Albie.
Albie who?
Albie very full after
this Christmas feast.

Knock, knock.
Who's there?
Canoe.
Canoe who?
Canoe smell all the Christmas food?

Knock, knock.
Who's there?
Alec.
Alec who?
Alec eggnog more than cocoa. Don't you?

Knock, knock.
Who's there?
Waiter.
Waiter who?
Waiter minute while everyone sits down for Christmas dinner.

Knock, knock.
Who's there?
Needle.
Needle who?
Needle little help to make Christmas cookies.

Knock, knock.
Who's there?
Sid.
Sid who?
Sid down. It's time for Christmas dinner!

Knock, knock.
Who's there?
Art.
Art who?
Art you ready yet for Christmas dinner?

Knock, knock.
Who's there?
Police.
Police who?
Police don't make me eat Brussels sprouts.

Knock, knock.
Who's there?
Pasta.
Pasta who?
Pasta stuffing, please.

Knock, knock.
Who's there?
Stan.
Stan who?
Stan back while I carve the turkey.

Knock, knock.
Who's there?
Possum.
Possum who?
Possum gravy on my turkey for me.

Knock, knock.
Who's there?
Homemade.
Homemade who?
Homemade the pie? It's delicious!

Knock, knock.
Who's there?
Alaska.
Alaska who?
Alaska again, would you like some more turkey?

Knock, knock.
Who's there?
Sand.
Sand who?
Sand us some Christmas cookies, please!

Knock, knock.
Who's there?
Sacha.
Sacha who?
Sacha an amazing selection of Christmas desserts!

Knock, knock.
Who's there?
Sherwood.
Sherwood who?
Sherwood like some more eggnog, please!

Knock, knock.
Who's there?
Wooden.
Wooden who?
Wooden you love some more pecan pie?

CHRISTMAS DINNER & FESTIVITIES

Knock, knock.
Who's there?
Yukon.
Yukon who?
Yukon have the rest of the figgy pudding.

Knock, knock.
Who's there?
Dozen.
Dozen who?
Dozen anyone want to try the Christmas cake?

Knock, knock.
Who's there?
Fangs.
Fangs who?
Fangs for the pie. It was delicious!

Knock, knock.
Who's there?
Aldo.
Aldo who?
Aldo anything for more figgy pudding.

Knock, knock.
Who's there?
Aida.
Aida who?
Aida lot of Christmas cookies.

Knock, knock.
Who's there?
Weekend.
Weekend who?
Weekend watch Christmas movies and sip hot cocoa.

CHRISTMAS DINNER & FESTIVITIES

Knock, knock.
Who's there?
Duncan.
Duncan who?
Duncan your Christmas cookies in milk is the best!

Knock, knock.
Who's there?
Irish.
Irish who?
Irish you a merry Christmas.

Knock, knock.
Who's there?
Canvas.
Canvas who?
Canvas Christmas Day get any better?

Knock, knock.
Who's there?
Mayor.
Mayor who?
Mayor Christmas be merry and bright.

NEW YEAR CELEBRATIONS

Knock, knock.
Who's there?
Dozen.
Dozen who?
Dozen this mean the year's almost over?

Knock, knock.
Who's there?
Taser.
Taser who?
Taser flying by quickly until New Year's.

Knock, knock.
Who's there?
You.
You who?
Wow, you're excited for New Year's!

Knock, knock.
Who's there?
Keith.
Keith who?
Keith me when the clock strikes twelve!

Knock, knock.
Who's there?
Counter.
Counter who?
Counter last ten seconds of the year.

Knock, knock.
Who's there?
Ima.
Ima who?
Ima counting down in 5, 4, 3, 2, 1.

Knock, knock.
Who's there?
Justin.
Justin who?
Justin time. We're starting the New Year countdown!

Knock, knock.
Who's there?
Razor.
Razor who?
Razor toast to a new year!

Knock, knock.
Who's there?
Abby.
Abby who?
Abby New Year everyone!

Knock, knock.
Who's there?
Cow.
Cow who?
Cow says, "Happy Moo Year!"

Knock, knock.
Who's there?
Ears.
Ears who?
Ears to a happy new year!

Knock, knock.
Who's there?
Otto.
Otto who?
This new year Otto be good.

WINTER FUN

Knock, knock.
Who's there?
Taco.
Taco who?
Taco bout a white Christmas!

Knock, knock.
Who's there?
Juicy.
Juicy who?
Juicy snow falling outside?

Knock, knock.
Who's there?
Joaquin.
Joaquin who?
"Joaquin in a winter wonderland."

Knock, knock.
Who's there?
Wendy.
Wendy who?
Wendy snow falls, we can make snow angels.

Knock, knock.
Who's there?
Theresa.
Theresa who?
Theresa all turning white from all the snow.

Knock, knock.
Who's there?
Youth.
Youth who?
Youth wanna paint snow outside with me?

Knock, knock.
Who's there?
Butch.
Butch who?
Butch your snow boots on.

Knock, knock.
Who's there?
Coin.
Coin who?
Coin I borrow your scarf?

Knock, knock.
Who's there?
Stopwatch.
Stopwatch who?
Stopwatch you're doing and come build a snowman!

Knock, knock.
Who's there?
Liar.
Liar who?
Liar the snow and make a snow angel.

Knock, knock.
Who's there?
Beet.
Beet who?
Beet me in a snowball fight.

Knock, knock.
Who's there?
Hal.
Hal who?
Hal about we go build a snow fort?

Knock, knock.
Who's there?
Hugo.
Hugo who?
Hugo on a sled ride with me?

Knock, knock.
Who's there?
Closure.
Closure who?
Closure jacket. It's freezing!

Knock, knock.
Who's there?
Sloth.
Sloth who?
Sloth my gloves. Can you help me find them?

Knock, knock.
Who's there?
Radio.
Radio who?
Radio for a snowball fight?

WINTER FUN

Knock, knock.
Who's there?
Ghost.
Ghost who?
Ghost faster! This sled needs to go faster!

Knock, knock.
Who's there?
Queen.
Queen who?
Queen the snow off the front porch before someone slips.

Knock, knock.
Who's there?
Cotton.
Cotton who?
Cotton a winter snowstorm. Send help!

Knock, knock.
Who's there?
Eiffel.
Eiffel who?
Eiffel in the snow, but I'm OK!

Knock, knock.
Who's there?
Flipper.
Flipper who?
Flipper sled, and you might get hurt.

Knock, knock.
Who's there?
Dragon.
Dragon who?
Dragon your sled through the snow is hard work.

Knock, knock.
Who's there?
Wire.
Wire who?
Wire you wearing shorts in the middle of winter?

Knock, knock.
Who's there?
Termite.
Termite who?
Termite get hurt if you slip on ice.

Knock, knock.
Who's there?
Stu.
Stu who?
Stu late to build a snowman. The snow has melted.

Knock, knock.
Who's there?
Sam.
Sam who?
Sam person who told you 206 other jokes.

BEFORE YOU GO

Did you have fun with those sometimes corny, Christmas knock-knock jokes?

Now that you have gotten the hang of knock-knock jokes, spend some time thinking up some of your own! Create your own jokes by thinking of some fun things you like about Christmas.

You can create jokes about Santa, Santa's elves and his reindeer, Christmas trees and decorations, Christmas stockings and presents, and traditions you enjoy on Christmas day.

Once you think up your own knock-knock jokes, you can play the game anywhere! It is a great game to play on long road trips, at school, or even when you are waiting in line at the store.

Have fun coming up with your own jokes and endless giggles!

WRITE YOUR OWN JOKES!

Have fun coming up with your own jokes and endless giggles!

WRITE YOUR OWN JOKES!

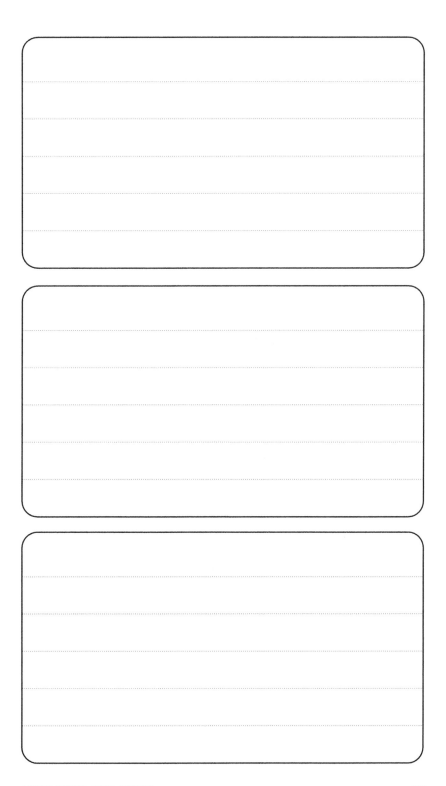

WRITE YOUR OWN JOKES!

WRITE YOUR OWN JOKES!

WRITE YOUR OWN JOKES!

WRITE YOUR OWN JOKES!

WRITE YOUR OWN JOKES!

WRITE YOUR OWN JOKES!

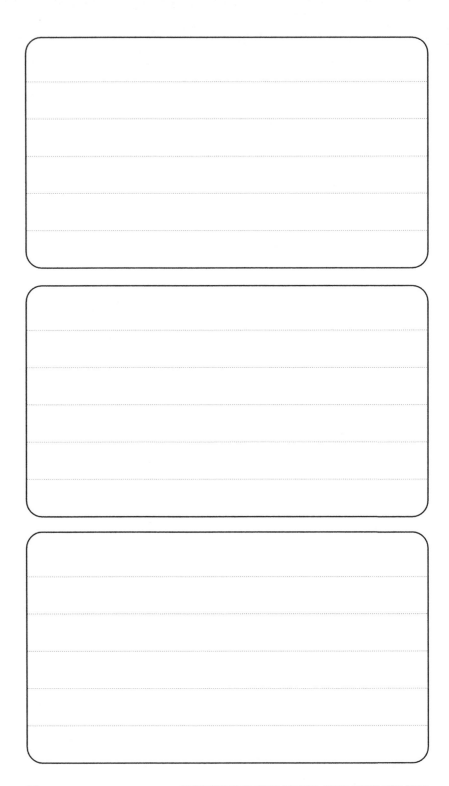

WRITE YOUR OWN JOKES!

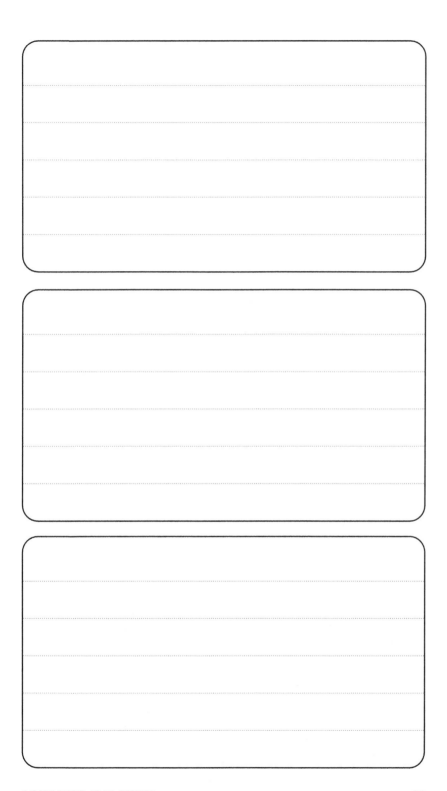

WRITE YOUR OWN JOKES!

COLLECT THEM ALL!

Christmas Would You Rather for Kids

Christmas Joke Book for Kids

Christmas Knock Knock Joke Book for Kids

www.riddlesandgiggles.com

REFERENCES

60 Christmas Knock Knock Jokes For Kids (n.d). Big Happy House. https://www.bighappyhouse.com/christmas-knock-knock-jokes-for-kids/

Christmas Knock Knock Jokes. (n.d). Funny Captions. http://www.funnycaptions.com/tag/christmas-knock-knock-jokes/4

Community, S. (2019, August 1). 80+ Funny Christmas Card Puns for the Holidays | Shutterfly. Ideas & Inspiration. https://www.shutterfly.com/ideas/christmas-card-puns/

Knock Knock Jokes - Funny Knock Knock Jokes. (n.d.). www.jokes4us.com http://www.jokes4us.com/knockknockjokes/index.html

Olivia. (2020, December 16), 50 Best Christmas Knock-Knock Jokes. This West Coast Mommy. https://thiswestcoastmommy.com/50-best-christmas-knock-knock-jokes/

Parent, B. (n.d.). Funny Puns and Punny Jokes: 100+ Hilarious Examples. https://examples.yourdictionary.com/examples-of-funny-puns-and-punny-funs.html

Made in the USA
Las Vegas, NV
18 December 2021